AF377917

The Johannine Priestly Model

Auto-édition : André Lagacé & Mireille Urlon-Lagacé

I am currently looking for a Catholic publisher to publish this document. If you meet this criterion and are interested in publishing it, please contact me at the following email address. If after two days you have not received a response, please contact my daughter at the second address:

andrelagace12@gmail.com
mireilleurlonlagace2684@hotmail.com

Version : January 2022

ISBN 978-2-9820629-2-4

Dépôt légal 1e trimestre 2022

Bibliothèque et Archives nationales du Québec
Bibliothèque et Archives Canada

André Lagacé

The Johannine priestly model

A priestly model for our time

I dedicate this booklet to the Virgin Mary.

My good mother, I place this writing at your feet. If what he announces is in accordance with your Son's will, please spread the message throughout the Church. Amen.

Table of contents

Introduction... 11

1- First explanation of the Jpm and
its institution 15
1.1- First explanation 15
1.2- The pattern of revelation in
Jn 19, 26-27..................................... 16
1.3- The original meaning of "Woman,
this is your son".................................. 18
1.4- The meaning of "This is your
mother" 20
1.5- Origin of the vocation of Mary to be
Mother of the Church........................ 22
1.6- Conclusion regarding the institution
of the Jpm... 25

2- The modalities of the Jpm 27
2.1- The wedding of Cana...................... 27
2.2- The unity of Jesus and Mary at
Golgotha 30

3- The reiteration of the Jpm 35
3.1- The meaning of the term "Woman" . 35
3.2- Rite and effects of the words in
Jn 19, 26-27..................................... 40
3.3- Access to the spiritual motherhood
of the Virgin Mary............................. 43
3.4- The evidence in favor of the
reiteration... 46
3.5- In order to avoid the risk of scandal. 50
3.6- The two pillars............................... 51

4- Various 53
   4.1- Spiritual formation and its
        importance 53
   4.2- Spiritual direction and vocational
        discernment 55
   4.3- An ombudsman for the protection
        of seminarians 58

Conclusion 59

Bibliography of the author 61

Introduction

In the course of the centuries, the people of God has always been able to count on the precious help of the Blessed Mother of God who, through her motherly intercession, has never ceased to bring considerable assistance to the Church of her divine Son. I am thinking here, among other things, of the scapular which she gave to saint Simon Stock, an English monk, and of the holy rosary. These are very precious aids that the Church has filially welcomed, not hesitating to make them sacramentals.

Now, in these times, a time when Western societies and families are being hit hard by an unprecedented secularization, causing a drastic break in the transmission of the faith, so that our churches are closing one after the other; in these times, too, when the Church is under constant internal and external pressure to open up access to the ministerial priesthood to women, even though the tradition based on theology does not allow it; it should therefore come as no surprise that our good heavenly mother is once again offering us help adapted to the times we are living through.

This help consists in the marvelous and unexpected gift of her motherhood within the Divine Will. A gift that she wishes to offer to women so that they may become mothers to her Son and love him as much as she loved him, «wanting to form many mothers to her

Jesus, to make him safe and so that no one offends him anymore [1]».

This access within the spirituality of the Divine Will to the motherhood of Mary allows us to discover that the particular priestly model of the Apostle John was intended to allow the ministry of the spiritual motherhood of the Virgin Mary to be exercised within the early Church and the Church of our time.

I strongly invite the readers, who will read the arguments presented below, to acquire a knowledge of this spirituality [2], because the gift of the Divine Will and the access to Mary's maternity that it makes possible can truly engender the Church to a new era; an era where the Will of God will be done on earth as it is in heaven; an era that the Church has asked for and asked for again and again within the Our Father for more than two thousand years; without fully understanding the deep meaning of this request.

Furthermore, knowledge of this spirituality will allow readers to understand that an adequate integration of this spirituality, on the part of those who would be destined to this priestly model, would greatly preserve them from the risks of corruption or scandal to which they could be subjected without this strong spirituality.

The present document contains four sections:

The first begins by giving an initial explanation of this priestly model; then it indicates how it was instituted.

The second explores the modalities of this model. The analysis of the episode of the wedding at

---

1- L. PICCARRETA, XXXIV, December 28, 1936.
2- There are several good introductory books on this spirituality on the market. A brief search will suffice to find them.

Cana and of the unity of Jesus and Mary on Calvary help to bring them out.

The third section deals with the question of the reiteration of this priestly model, which makes it possible to discover by virtue of what authority it is possible to reiterate it.

I conclude by addressing the spiritual formation and spiritual direction of seminarians who might one day be destined to this priestly model.

Before moving on to the first part, I wish to declare that I submit myself in advance to the judgment that the Church's Magisterium might one day make on what I am saying. I would also like to add that my mother tongue is French and I am far from mastering English, so I beg forgiveness if there are any gross errors in this translation. At the time I translate these lines, my days are numbered and I am with few resources. Since what the Lord has given me to discover has not yet attracted attention, I preferred to translate with linguistic errors rather than die without having tried everything to make known this marvelous novelty for our time. May the Lord bless you!

1

First explanation of the Jpm
and its institution

This section provides an initial understanding of the Johannine priestly model. Having gained this understanding, I will indicate how this priestly model was instituted by Christ on the cross. To do this, I will manifest the pattern of revelation present in Jn 19:26-27. The highlighting of this pattern will allow us to understand that the institution of this priestly model results from the establishment of three vocations.

1.1– First explanation

As its name indicates, the Johannine priestly model consists in the priestly model of the apostle John. Indeed, this apostle having lived his priesthood in connection with the Virgin Mary, mother of God and of the Church, he has a priestly model different from that of other apostles, bishops or priests in the history of the Church.

Why did the apostle John live his priesthood in close relationship with the Virgin Mary? Because Christ on the cross entrusted his mother to his filial protection through the words: "Woman, this is your son" and "This is your mother". He took her into his home as a son takes care of his mother, if she is without resources or protection. However, this was not a natural filiation, but a filiation in the order of grace..

Of course, each of us has been called to welcome Mary as a mother in the order of grace, but none of us, unlike the apostle John, has been given the responsibility to ensure her physical protection and general well-being. A responsibility that finds its expression in the phrase from the gospel in Jn 19: 27: "From that hour the disciple welcomed him into his home."

From this responsibility entrusted to the apostle John, it follows that Mary exercised the ministry of her spiritual motherhood within the early Church in conjunction with him; which was part of a mysterious design of the Divine Will.

Indeed, in his omniscience, the Lord knew that his mother would give access to his divine and spiritual motherhood within the Divine Will. Just as he knew that through this access it would be possible for women to exercise the ministry of the spiritual motherhood of his mother within the Church. He saw all this in view of our time, for he revealed this spirituality to the Italian mystic Luisa Piccarreta from 1899 to 1938.

Knowing this, it becomes easy to understand that he instituted this priestly model in such a way that it could be repeated; this in order to allow women, who will be called by God to this end, to exercise this ministry of this motherhood.

What is the ministry of the spiritual motherhood of the Virgin Mary and what is its purpose? These are questions that I intend to answer in the next few sections. However, for the moment, let us look at the question of the institution of this priestly model.

1.2– The pattern of revelation in Jn 19, 26–27

In John's gospel, when the action of seeing is followed by the action of saying, we are generally in the presence of a pattern of revelation. The author of the fourth gospel uses this literary device to mean that

John the Baptist or Christ Jesus reveals the vocation of the one who is seen or looked at.

Here are two examples where this pattern is used. To highlight its use, I bold the key words of seeing and saying and underline the vocation that is thus revealed.

The first example is found in Jn 1:35-36 where we read:

> *On the following day as John stood there again with two of his disciples, Jesus passed, and **John stares hard at him and said**, 'Look, there is the lamb of God'.*

(Jérusalem Bible, Jn 1, 35-36)

And, a few verses later, we have in Jn 1, 42:

> *And he took Simon to Jesus. **Jesus looked hard at him and said**, 'You are Simon son of John; you are to be called Cephas' - meaning Rock.*

These two examples illustrate beautifully that this scheme is a revealer of vocation.

Now, if we turn our attention to the words that are at the basis of the institution of the Johannine priestly model, we will see the presence of this pattern:

> ***Seeing his mother and the disciple he loved** standing near her, Jesus **said to his mother**, 'Woman, this is your son'. Then **to the disciple he said**, 'This is your mother'. And from that moment the disciple made a place for her in his home.*

(Jn 19, 26-27)

We will begin by looking at the first two vocations that result from Christ's first sentence, that is, within the "Woman, this is your son."

1.3– The original meaning of "Woman, this is your son"

In order to interpret the sentence "Woman, this is your son" properly, we must distinguish between the literal and the spiritual meaning.

The literal meaning implies that Jesus was Mary's only child and that, without him, his mother was without family protection, more specifically filial protection.

The tenderness of his filial love for his mother therefore prompted him to provide her with protection. But this was not the only thing at stake, for in doing so he was also obeying the will of his heavenly Father who was calling him, at the very moment he entrusted his mother to his beloved disciple, to grant the latter a priestly model different from that of the other apostles.

The fact that Christ Jesus personally entrusted his mother to the apostle John with the words "Woman, this is your son" is well known and is part of the tradition. John Paul II only takes up this tradition when he writes in the encyclical Redemptoris Mater:

The Redeemer entrusts his mother to the disciple, and at the same time he gives her to him as his mother.

Pope JOHN PAUL II, *Redemptoris Mater*, 45.

The Redeemer therefore entrusted his mother to John, but since she is the mother of all his disciples and therefore also the mother of this apostle in the order of grace, this meant that he had to take on this vocation as a son shelters and takes care of his mother if she is without protection or support. Thus, by virtue of the "Woman, this is your son", the vocation to filially assume the charge of the mother of his beloved Master was added to that which he had as an apostle.

In the same paragraph of the above-mentioned encyclical, the Polish pope specifies that the sentence "And from that hour the disciple took her to his own home" "indicates, even though indirectly, everything expressed by the intimate relationship of a child with its mother." "And since Mary was given as a mother to him personally", John felt called to give himself up to her in a filial way and thus to welcome her into his home.

Thus, within the intimate filial relationship he developed with Mary, because he welcomed her into his home, that is, into his personal possessions, John becomes an analogy for each of us. An analogy to follow in order to live well the Marian dimension of our discipleship. This is what John Paul II indicates when he writes:

> *Entrusting himself to Mary in a filial manner, the Christian, like the Apostle John, « Welcomes » the Mother of Christ "into his own home" and brings her into everything that makes up his inner life, that is to say into his human and Christian "I": he "took her to his own home.".*

> *Ibid.*

It can also be inferred that John's reverent filial relationship with the Virgin Mary, as they jointly carried out their respective ministries in the early Church, invited all of the Lord's disciples to establish a similar filial relationship with Mary, a relationship which they naturally extended to their interior life after her Assumption.

As we shall see in subsection 1.5 below, the words "Woman, this is your son" do not ground Mary in her vocation as Mother of the Church, but they manifest how this vocation must be exercised, that is, under John's protection; which allowed her to exercise her spiritual motherhood within the early Church in connection with him. This is the first element that distinguishes the Johannine priestly model from other priestly models.

In conclusion, I would say that the primary meaning of "Woman, this is your son" is the literal meaning, and that it is only from this primary meaning that an analogy can unfold, in a second stage, for the whole of us members of the Church.

1.4– The meaning of "This is your mother"

In order to determine the meaning of "This is your mother", it is necessary to verify whether it has another purpose than that of a formal presentation; a presentation that can be represented by the following example: "My son, this is your sister", "My daughter, this is your brother".

Unlike "Woman, this is your son" where the term "Woman" refers to the recipient of this word, there is no recipient mentioned in the sentence: "This is your mother." The absence of an addressee within this second sentence causes a dissonance, an anomaly in relation to the first; this takes us out of the framework of a harmonious conventional presentation.

The absence of an addressee within a word of Christ can mean that he addresses it to all. Some will object that he could also have used the term "son" or "child" to address our vocation as children of Mary in the order of grace.

Perhaps Christ Jesus could have addressed our vocation using the term "son," which would have read, "Son, this is your mother." However, although it is an anonymous term, it refers to a male child. It would therefore be an inappropriate term to use as an archetypal term for the entire Church, which is composed of men and women.

The term "child" has the advantage of being gender neutral, which would have been "Child, this is your mother". This term would have been a more appropriate archetypal term to address our vocation as children of Mary in Christ, but it is still infantilizing.

However, using the term "son" or "child" would have created some ambiguity. It would have been unclear whether Christ Jesus was addressing this word only to John or to each of his disciples.

Thus, in order to make this part of the revelatory scheme address the whole Church, the best alternative was to omit the mention of an addressee. And this is precisely what Christ Jesus did.

What must we conclude from this? We must conclude that the sentence "This is your mother", in accordance with the constant teaching of the Church, is addressed to the entire people of the New Covenant and even to the whole of humanity, because it reveals to those who listen to Christ their vocation to be the spiritual daughter or son of the Virgin Mary.

1.5– Origin of the vocation of Mary to be the Mother of the Church

Mary's unique place within the Church derives from her vocation to be the mother of Christ. In fact, it is from this primary vocation that also derives that of being the mother of his mystical body. It is therefore with good reason that it is possible to attribute to Mary the title of "Mother of the Church".

The simplest way to find the origin of Mary's vocation to be the Mother of the Church is undoubtedly that of analogy. To do this, let us ask ourselves the following question: when does the vocation of motherhood become a fact in a woman?

I believe that the answer to this question is when she learns or discovers that she is pregnant. Generally, the child is only an embryo, but she is nevertheless the mother of that embryo. Her vocation as a mother begins at that moment.

Consequently, this analogy invites us not to seek the foundation of Mary's vocation to be the mother of the mystical body of Christ at the moment of the birth of the Church. A birth that some theologians place at the cross, when Christ's side was pierced by the lance, and others at Pentecost.

Mary learned of her vocation to be the mother of Christ at the Annunciation, at the announcement of the Archangel Gabriel, and she consented to the conception of Christ in her by her fiat. Since it is impossible to separate the head from the body, this is also where we must place the beginning of the Church, even if it is embryonic.

This last statement is in perfect conformity with the liturgy through which the Church expresses her mystery. Indeed, as the prayer on the offerings that the

Church addresses each year to Almighty God on the feast of the Annunciation indicates:

Accept, Almighty God, the gifts offered by your Church: she does not forget that she began the day your Word became flesh; grant us, on this feast of the Annunciation, to celebrate with joy the mysteries of Christ. He who.

English translation of the French prayer [1]
of Missel de la semaine (2014). Paris,
Mame-Desclée, p.1701-1702.

We can easily agree that the vocation to be the Mother of the Church carries with it an enormous responsibility. And, to return to our analogy, even if the vocation of mother or father is sometimes imposed on them, it is no less true that this vocation should require informed consent.

The same is true for the vocation of Mother of the Church. The Lord's love and respect for her perfect servant implies that he asked her consent for this vocation as well, so as not to impose it on her.

Therefore, in order for her to give the Archangel Gabriel her informed consent, it was essential that she knew that accepting to be the mother of Christ also implied being the mother of his mystical body.

Being the Immaculate Conception, the Virgin Mary possessed the gift of infused wisdom; a gift she possessed in fullness, since this gift was never altered either by original sin or by personal sins. By virtue of this gift, it was easy for her to understand that being

---

1 Daigne accepter, Dieu tout-puissant, les dons offerts par ton Église : elle n'oublie pas qu'elle a commencé le jour où ton Verbe s'est fait chair; accorde-nous, en cette fête de l'Annonciation, de célébrer avec joie les mystères du Christ. Lui qui.

the Mother of Christ also implied being the Mother of his mystical body.

Therefore, the fiat to the divine motherhood was also a fiat to the spiritual motherhood that was connected to it. I believe that this statement of Isaac of Stella is directly addressed to the Virgin Mary within the mystery of the Annunciation. Isaac of Stella is a twelfth-century Cistercian theologian monk:

> *Be careful not to separate the head from the body; do not prevent Christ from existing as a whole; for Christ does not exist anywhere as a whole without the Church, nor the Church without Christ. The total, integral Christ is the head and the body.*

> English translation of the sermon by Isaac of stella. [2] Liturgie des heures IV. Temps ordinaire 23e semaine.

In view of what Christ revealed to the Italian mystic Luisa Piccarreta, the affirmation of Isaac of Stella and that of the Church's liturgy, which allow us to situate the origin of Mary's vocation as Mother of the Church at the Annunciation, could not be more correct. In fact, in The Book of Heaven, volume 12, on January 10, 1921, Christ Jesus states to Luisa Piccarreta, regarding the fiat that Mary pronounced at the Annunciation:

> *As soon as She said, 'FIAT MIHI', not only did She take possession of Me, but She overshadowed all creatures and all created things. She felt within Herself the life of all creatures, and from that moment She began to act as the Mother and Queen of all. How many portents does this*

---

2 Garde-toi bien de séparer la tête du corps; n'empêche pas le Christ d'exister tout entier; car le Christ n'existe nulle part tout entier sans l'Église, ni l'Église sans le Christ. Le Christ total, intégral, c'est la tête et le corps.

'yes' of my Mama not contain – if I wanted to tell them all, you would never stop listening.

The Virgin Mary would therefore have embraced her vocation as Mother and Queen of all immediately after the proclamation of her fiat. We can deduce that her vocation as Mother of the Church is so closely linked to that of her divine motherhood that it was implied or included in the latter.

Thus, the "Woman, this is your son" is not the origin of Mary's vocation to be the Mother of the Church, but the call to exercise the ministry of that vocation within the nascent Church in close connection with John.

1.6– Conclusion regarding the institution of the Jpm

The analysis of the pattern of revelation present in Jn 19, 26-27 has allowed me to identify three vocations: the first two are addressed to John and Mary, and the third is addressed to each member of humanity who receives this word of Christ.

Within this scheme, the Virgin Mary is seen with the disciple whom Jesus loved beside her. She is the spiritual mother whom Christ on the cross entrusts to all the members of humanity with the word: "This is your mother", so that they may introduce her as their mother into the order of grace "in the whole space of their interior life". It is therefore up to us to accept this vocation that is addressed to us.

As for the priest who is seen, because he stands close to her, in addition to the vocation that is addressed to all, there is the vocation to introduce the one who stands close to him among his personal possessions, like a son welcomes his mother into his home, because the one he welcomes is his mother in Christ Jesus.

Finally, there is the vocation of the woman who is entrusted. To her vocation to exercise the ministry of her spiritual motherhood among the disciples of the Lord is added that of living under the filial protection of the priest who stands beside her, while having with him a relationship that is all maternal since he is one of her sons in his Son.

Now that the foundation of this priestly model has been manifested through the analysis of the vocations contained in the pattern of vocation: "Woman, this is your son" and "This is your mother", it is appropriate to discover the specific modalities that revelation gives us for this very particular priestly model.

2

The modalities of the Jpm

In this section, I will begin by presenting the major pastoral orientations of the Johannine priestly model. This will be done with the help of the gospel episode of the Wedding at Cana. In a second step, I will deepen the particular modalities that those who are destined to the Johannine priestly model will have to embrace in order to properly fulfill their vocation. I will do this by studying the modalities that determined the unity of Jesus and Mary at Golgotha.

Why did I choose these two Gospel episodes to discover the pastoral orientations of the Johannine priestly model and the particular modalities that those who might one day be destined to this priestly model are called to embrace? I chose them because they are the only two episodes where Jesus and Mary exercise their respective ministry together.

Please note that I will refer to the priests who, for the purposes of this paper, will be included in this particular priestly model as "little Johns". As for the women I will fictitiously integrate into this model, I will refer to them as "little Marys". I will indicate below the reason for these denominations.

2.1– The wedding of Cana

In this story, Jesus is invited with his disciples to a wedding. Jesus' mother is also present, and when the wedding wine runs out, she tells her son, "They have no wine". Then she adds to the wedding servants, "Whatever he tells you, do it."

Jesus then asks them to fill the six stone jars with water. Once the jars were full, he ordered them to draw water and take it to the master of the meal. The latter tastes the water turned into wine and, without knowing the origin of the wine, praises the groom for having kept the good wine throughout the wedding.

This evangelical episode has a precise symbolism: the exhausted wine means that the Old Covenant with its animal sacrifices has come to an end. The water changed into new wine represents the New Covenant between God and humans; a covenant that transforms the celebrations into a divine wedding.

By generously making up for exhausted wine, turning water into wine, Christ Jesus acts as a true father to both the bride and groom and to the families gathered for the wedding. This is not unrelated to the symbolism of this story. Indeed, by providing the sacrifice of the New Covenant, he brought to completion the revelation of the Father's love for the world, thus becoming the most perfect icon of it.

Even if Christ can bear the messianic title of Father-Eternal (Is 9, 5) because he is consubstantial with the Father, his identity is marked by a spiritual fatherhood that is even more immediate for us, a fatherhood that was expressed through his proclamation of the Gospel and the sacrifice of his life. Indeed, it is through these various elements that he regenerates humanity to the divine life.

By assuming this spiritual fatherhood of Christ in the Divine Will, the little Johns will be able to share his fatherly feelings towards past, present and future humanity. Thus, the gift of themselves within their priestly ministry will be all the more complete.

As for the saving and sanctifying power of their ministry, it will be considerably increased, because their actions (thoughts, looks, prayers, words, gestures, etc.) will be assumed, divinized and multiplied for all by Christ Jesus within the Divine Fiat. They will have the same value as if it were Christ himself who performed them.

The text of the wedding feast of Cana thus invites us to see in the little Johns ministers of the New Covenant, but ministers who will exercise their pastoral ministry in union with their little Mary within the families. The ardent and supernatural parental solicitude that they will have for families and for each of their members will allow them to bring them fully into this new covenant.

With regard to the objective of evangelization that the Johannine priestly model is called to carry out within families, it will have as its goal to transform them, according to the wish expressed in the Second Vatican Council, into domestic Churches; that is, into places where the word of God is proclaimed and meditated upon daily, so that they may fully experience the joys of the Gospel and live in the Divine Will, so that God's will be done on earth as it is in Heaven.

The pastoral ministry of the Johannine priestly model consists, therefore, in going to meet families, evangelizing them (introducing them to the New Covenant), catechizing them, initiating them to live and do "oratio" in the Divine Will. To this is added the spiritual direction of women and girls for little Mary and the spiritual direction of men and boys for little John.

2.2– The unity of Jesus and Mary at Golgotha

Of the four evangelists, John is the only one to mention the presence of Mary, mother of Jesus, at Golgotha. This is the episode where Christ, raised on the cross, seeing his mother and the disciple he loved beside her, declares to her: "Woman, this is your son" and then declares to this same disciple: "This is your mother."

Obviously, these two sentences do not adequately define the unity of Jesus and Mary during their common passion on Golgotha. In order to bring out this unity, I will have recourse to a text taken from the eighth chapter of the Dogmatic Constitution on the Church of the Second Vatican Council; this chapter aims to situate the Virgin Mary, Mother of God, in the mystery of Christ and of the Church:

> *After this manner the Blessed Virgin advanced in her pilgrimage of faith, and faithfully persevered in her union with her Son unto the cross, where she stood, in keeping with the divine plan, grieving exceedingly with her only begotten Son, uniting herself with a maternal heart with His sacrifice, and lovingly consenting to the immolation of this Victim which she herself had brought forth.*

Vatican II, *Lumen Gentium*, 58.

Thus, the unity of Christ and the Virgin Mary is manifested in an incomparable way at the cross, because she associated herself with a maternal heart to his sacrifice; a sacrifice to which she consented in cruel suffering.

If Mary was able to give the consent of her love to the immolation of her divine Son, whom she loved more than anything else, it was because she had the feelings of a true mother towards us. Only parents are ready to sacrifice everything for the salvation of their children, even if it means losing their lives or having their hearts pierced by a sword of pain.

Knowing that our souls in exile needed a human mother filled with solicitude, the Holy Trinity made her the maternal pole of our regeneration in Christ, which made Christ say to Luisa Piccarreta that all the goods acquired by his passion, that is to say:

> *Therefore, there is no grace that descends upon earth, there is no Sanctity that is formed, there is no sinner that is converted, there is no Love that departs from Our throne, which is not deposited in Her Heart of Mother first; and She forms the maturation of that good, She fecundates it with Her Love, She enriches it with Her graces and, if needed, with the Virtue of Her sorrows; and then She deposits it in the one who must receive it, in such a way that the creature who receives it feels the Divine Paternity and the Maternity of her Celestial Mother.*

L. PICCARRETA, XXXIV, December 8, 1935.

Moreover, in this same volume, we learn that Mary, from her conception, was the heiress of the Divine Fiat and that the trinitarian love…

> *[…] made this Virgin to be conceived in each creature, so that each one might have a Mother all for himself, and they might feel Her Maternity, Her Love, in the depth of their souls, such that, while She keeps them conceived within Herself, as more than Her own children, bilocating Herself, She is conceived in each creature, to place Herself at their disposal,*

to raise them, guide them, free them from dangers, and with Her maternal Power, feed them the Milk of Her Love and the Food with which She Herself is nourished-that is, the Divine Fiat.

L. PICCARRETA, XXXIV, December 20, 1936.

Not only does she motherly watch over each of her children, but she is also the one who generates Jesus in each of them:

First You Must Know that this Celestial Queen, by possessing all the fullness of Our Divine Fiat-which possesses by Its own nature the generative and bilocating Virtue-together with the Divine Fiat She can generate and bilocate Her Son-God as many times as She wants. And so Our Love imposes Itself on this Celestial Creature and, delirious, by virtue of My Fiat that She possessed, gives Her the Power to generate Her Jesus in each creature; She makes Him be born, She nurtures Him, She does for the creature everything that is needed in order to form the Life of Her dear Son. She makes up for all that the creature does not do for Him [...]

L. PICCARRETA, XXXIV, December 24, 1936.

In the light of these teachings which Christ Jesus transmitted to us through the Italian mystic Luisa Piccarreta, it is easy to see the universal paternity of Christ and the universal maternity of Mary behind the person of Christ and that of his mother at the wedding in Cana and at Golgotha.

These teachings also allow us to understand that it is in virtue of the Divine Will that they are able to exercise this spiritual fatherhood and motherhood respectively with regard to all. It is not surprising, therefore, that the spirituality of the Divine Will is indispensable to the Johannine priestly model.

In light of this unity and the spiritual parenthood that Christ Jesus and his mother exercise at the wedding at Cana and at the cross, it becomes clear that little Johns must embrace the spiritual fatherhood of Christ Jesus and little Marys the spiritual motherhood of the Virgin Mary. This within the spirituality of the Divine Will.

It is by reiterating day after day their consecration to the Divine Will and by embracing unceasingly this fatherhood or motherhood within this Will that they are called to die to their small human will in order to live only in the Divine Will.

3

The reiteration of the Jpm

Now that we have learned about the modalities of the Johannine priestly model, it is appropriate to address the question of its reiteration.

To do this, I will explore the meaning of the term "Woman" that Christ used in reference to his mother at the wedding in Cana and at Golgotha. I will then indicate the effect of the words "Woman, this is your son" and "This is your mother" if they were used in a non-sacramental rite, thus allowing us to discover the authority by which this priestly model could be repeated.

I will conclude by pointing to two very compelling clues in the Gospel that the Lord wants his Church to take advantage of the Johannine priestly model.

3.1– The meaning of the term "Woman"

It is quite legitimate to be surprised by the solemn "Woman" that Jesus used to address his mother at Golgatha. It is a terribly cold and impersonal term, given the tragic and painful situation in which they both found themselves.

The traditional interpretation explains Christ's use of this word as a reference to the proto-gospel where it is written:

I will make you enemies of each other: you and the woman, your offspring and her offspring. It will crush your head and you will strike its heel'.

(Gn 3, 15)

I do not blame the biblical commentators for promoting this interpretation, which, by the way, is not wrong. However, this was not the primary reason for the use of the term "Woman". In fact, until recently, it was not the time for the Church to enter into a proper understanding of Christ's use of this term for his mother; the Johannine priestly model was intended only for our time.

To understand that the term "Woman" is not primarily a reference to the proto-gospel, it is sufficient to understand that Christ's identity as universal Redeemer was fully manifested on the cross. Indeed, the prophet Isaiah had described the suffering servant in sufficient detail for the Israelites of good will, who had witnessed the divine words and works of Christ Jesus, and who now saw him lifted up on the cross, to understand that he was the Messiah, the Anointed One of God.

It was therefore obvious that he was the son of the woman and that the woman who had given birth to him was the woman of the proto-gospel. So what was fully manifested did not need to be recalled. Therefore, Christ's intention in using the term "woman" in "Woman, this is your son" was rather to ensure that the priestly model of the disciple he loved could be reiterated.

Indeed, if he had addressed his mother as he was accustomed to do in everyday life by saying, for example, "Mother (or Mama), this is your your son," John would have continued to enjoy a very special priestly model, but his priestly model could not have been reiterated, since the term "Mother" or "Mama" would have limited the scope of this word only to his mother.

However, by saying: "Woman, this is your son", the term "Woman", in the context of a ritual word intended by him, in order to reiterate the priestly model of the apostle John, can be addressed to women other than Mary, because it is a feminine generic.

Some will object that this term cannot testify to such an intention on his part, since he addressed his mother with this same term at the wedding in Cana, thus implying that he regularly addressed his mother in this way.

This is a hasty conclusion, for if Christ knew from the beginning of his ministry that he was going to institute the Johannine priestly model on the cross through the words "Woman, this is your son" and "This is your mother" then his use of the term "woman" to his mother at the wedding at Cana could mean that he was addressing, through his mother, those women who were destined to take part in the Johannine priestly model.

And why would he address them? To teach them that they will not be able to use the natural authority that mothers have over their children in relation to their son-priest. To demonstrate that this teaching is indeed present in the episode of the wedding at Cana, I will quote the following verses from this episode:

Three days later there was a wedding at Cana in Galilee. The mother of Jesus was there, and Jesus and his disciples had also been invited. When they ran out of wine, since the wine provided for the wedding was all finished, the mother of Jesus said to him, 'They have no wine'. Jesus said 'Woman, why turn to me? My hour has not come yet.'

(Jn 2, 1-4)

As we can see, in response to his mother's implicit request that the wine for the wedding be used up, the Lord answers her in a way that seems both shocking and haughty: "Woman, why turn to me? My hour has not come yet."

The expression "Why turn to me?" is the translation of a Semitic expression which is literally formulated as follows: "What is mine and yours?" The contemporaries of Jesus used this expression to refuse a request that they considered inappropriate. This one is all the more abrupt and shocking in the mouth of the Lord because he was addressing it to his own mother who was always of perfect charity and not to a sinful woman.

In fact, the Lord, who had perfectly understood that his mother was referring to the lack of wine for the wedding feast, pretended to have heard in her request: «they have no wine", a request for the wine of the New Covenant and, to explain his refusal to this alleged request, he declares: "My hour has not yet come."

It goes without saying that this request from Mary would have been quite premature, since he was only at the beginning of his public ministry. He therefore signifies his refusal by answering her, "What is mine and yours, woman?"

By refusing to comply with this allegedly untimely request - I say "allegedly", since it was cleverly staged by himself - he thus teaches the future little Marys, who find themselves in the "woman" he addressed to his mother, that the little Johns will be released from their duty of filial obedience to them, for they will have to be, like their Master, entirely given to their mission.

In fact, through the "What is mine and yours, woman?", it is as if he were saying to his mother, in order to teach the future little Marys: "Before, as a son should, I obeyed your every wish. However, now that the Father has called me to work in his vineyard, I must be totally dedicated to my mission."

Thus, by this apparent refusal, he makes it clear that he is released from his duty of filial obedience to his mother. And as Mary was subordinated to her Son from the moment he began his public ministry, the latter being henceforth the Master (the Rabbi), it is right that the little Marys should be subordinate to their priest-son who is a visible extension of Christ in his priestly being.

I am of the opinion that it is fortunate that this is so, for this disposition and the thoughtful love that little John and little Mary will have for each other, in the Divine Will, will enable them to be models for the spouses to imitate.

In fact, as husbands must be, by their love and the exercise of their holy authority towards their wives and children, a sacramental sign of Christ's love for his Church, the latter will easily be able to take as a model the authority and the tender and considerate love that their little John will have towards their little Mary; little Mary in whom little John and Christian families will revere as a sign of the presence of the Virgin Mary among them.

The same goes for the wives who must be, by their tender and thoughtful love for their husbands, a sacramental sign of the Church's love for Christ. They can take as a model their little Mary who, while recognizing the authority of her son-priest over her, will revere the presence of Christ in him.

Now that Jesus' use of the term "Woman" in relation to his mother is clarified, let us consider the effect that the words "Woman, this is your son" and "This is your mother" might have within a rite for the reiteration of this priestly model.

3.2– Rite and effects of the words in Jn 19, 26–27

Before beginning this section on the reiteration of the Johannine priestly model, I find it important to specify at the outset that I will not use the term "sacrament" but rather the term "rite" or "ritual" for its reiteration.

Indeed, there are only seven sacraments, no more and no less. The Magisterium of the Church was very clear about this at the Council of Trent. Thus, this rite of reiteration would have effect only in virtue of the power that bishops receive at their episcopal ordination, namely the power to bind and loose.

In virtue of the chaste binomial John and Mary, the subject of this rite would be a religious ordained as priest or bishop and a nun. I will explain below why I recommend very strongly that the candidates for this priestly model be religious men and women from the same community.

Let us therefore fictitiously place this religious ordained as a priest and this nun in the presence of a bishop. In this rite, the bishop represents Christ on the cross, the ordained minister becomes a sign of the apostle John, and the consecrated woman makes the Virgin Mary present to the spirit of the People of God, witness to the rite.

The bishop lays his hands on them and then declares to the nun at the end of a consecratory prayer: "Woman, this is your son."

With these words, the bishop entrusts this consecrated woman who assumes the spiritual motherhood of the Virgin Mary in the Divine Fiat to the priest who, standing beside her, welcomes her as a son welcomes his mother into his home. He welcomes her so that she may exercise, in conjunction with him, the ministry of the spiritual motherhood of the Virgin Mary to the families entrusted to him.

Thus, in virtue of this rite, this nun becomes a sacramental of the Virgin Mary for this priest and his community. She could therefore be referred to as the "little Mary". As for this priest who would become in virtue of this rite a sacramental of Saint John, he could then be designated under the term "little John".

Then, turning to this priest, the bishop would declare to him, "This is your mother." As mentioned above, the "This is your mother" is addressed both to the little John, who receives her as his mother into his personal possessions, and to the people of God present, who represent all the members of the People of God, so that they may welcome her as a minister of Mary.

On the one hand, this rite is based on the ability of a bishop to bind and unbind, a power that Christ used on the cross by binding John and Mary and which he transmitted to his apostles and their successors. On the other hand, this same rite requires the authority of bishops to give pastoral mandates for the fulfillment of a pastoral office within their diocese.

Thus, if the Holy See ever authorizes the reiteration of the Johannine priestly model, a bishop after the celebration of this rite would have the right to give this nun a pastoral mandate; that is to exercise the pastoral office of the ministry of the spiritual motherhood of the Virgin Mary within his diocese.

As for the rite itself, it could be a rite of consecration similar to that of the virgins except that, in this case, it would be the rite of consecration to the Johannine priestly model. A rite where the priest and the nun, after being questioned by the bishop, would be called to make or renew their vow of perpetual chastity. This done, the bishop could proclaim the consecratory prayer to the Johannine priestly model which ended with the words, "Woman, this is your son" and "This is your mother."

Thus, in virtue of this rite of consecration to the Johannine priestly model, the ordained minister would become, in addition to being a sacramental sign of Christ, a sacramental of the presence of the apostle John. As for the nun, she would become a sacramental of the Virgin Mary; this in virtue of her vow of chastity and her consecration to the Johannine priestly model for the exercise of the ministry of the motherhood of Mary.

Mother Church has the power to institute a sacramental according to the needs of the people of God at a given time. In this case, it would be to respond to the needs of Christian families which, hit hard by the unprecedented secularization of Western societies, once Christian, are falling into ruin, so that they are practically no longer places of transmission of the faith.

That being said, in the absence of authentic access to the spiritual motherhood of the Virgin Mary, it would be ridiculous to give little Mary's the mandate to exercise the ministry of her spiritual motherhood. It is therefore appropriate to address this point without delay.

3.3– Access to the spiritual motherhood of the Virgin Mary

I have indicated above that access to the spiritual motherhood of the Virgin Mary is realized within the spirituality of the Divine Will.

Here is the text on which I base my demonstration of this access. It comes from the work entitled: The Book of Heaven. A work that contains 36 volumes; a work where Christ reveals the spirituality of the Divine Will through the Italian mystic Luisa Piccarreta:

Now, in this inheritance of the Fiat She inherited the Fecundity, the Maternity, human and Divine; She inherited the Word of the Celestial Father; She inherited all human generations, and these will inherit all the Goods of this Celestial Mother.

"Therefore, as Her heirs, and as their Mother, She has the right to generate Her children in Her Maternal Heart. But this was not enough to Our Love and to Hers-She wanted to generate in each creature, and since She is the Heiress of the Divine Word, She has the Power to have Him generated in each of them. How? If evils, passions, weaknesses, can be inherited, why should it not be possible to inherit the Goods? And this is why the Celestial Heiress wants to make known the Inheritance that She wants to give to Her children-She wants to give Her Maternity to the creatures, so that, as She generates Him, they may act as mamas to Him, and may Love Him as She Loved Him. She wants to form as many mamas for Her

Jesus in order to place Him in safety, and so that no one may offend Him any more. In fact, the Love of Mother is so very different from the other Loves; it is a Love that burns always, a Love that lays down its Life for its dear Son. See, She wants to endow the creature with Her Maternal Love and make them heirs of Her own Son. O! how honored She will feel in seeing that the creatures Love Her Jesus with Her same Love of Mother. You Must Know that Her Love toward Me and toward creatures is so great, that unable to contain It any longer, She Prayed Me to manifest to you what I have told you – Her great Inheritance; that She is waiting for Her heirs, and what She can do for them [...]

L. PICCARRETA, XXXIV, December 28, 1936.

By inheriting in the Divine Fiat of their heavenly mother, that is to say of her maternity and her maternal love towards her divine Son, the little Marys are called to take part in her maternity, both divine and spiritual. Thus, taking as their center Mary most holy who is conceived in their souls - this so that all creatures may have a mother all their own - the little Marys will love Jesus, their little John and all humanity with the maternal love present in Mary in the Divine Fiat.

As the spiritual motherhood of the Virgin Mary flows from her divine motherhood, by granting her heirs to inherit the latter, the grace of this same gift will also give them access to her spiritual motherhood; the one does not go without the other.

Indeed, just as it would be inappropriate to prevent Christ from existing as a whole by separating the head from the members, it would be equally inappropriate to prevent Mary from being a mother in her own right through her little Marys.

Let me quote again the statement of Isaac of Stella, for what he said of Christ can also be applied to Mary and her two maternities.

Let us begin by quoting his statement:

Be careful not to separate the head from the body; do not prevent Christ from existing as a whole; for Christ does not exist anywhere as a whole without the Church, nor the Church without Christ. The total, integral Christ is the head and the body.

English translation of the French version
by Isaac of Stella. ibid

Now, here is the application we can make of this wise quote for Mary and her spiritual motherhood:

Let us be careful not to separate the motherhood that Mary exercises in the place of the head from that which she exercises in the place of the body; let us not prevent Mary from being a mother in her own right in her little Marys; for Mary exists nowhere without the body of Christ, nor Christ without Mary. The total and integral motherhood of Mary is the divine motherhood in the place of the head and the spiritual motherhood in the place of the body.

This allows us to understand that it is not desirable or even conceivable for Christ to give access to Mary's divine maternity in the Divine Fiat, without simultaneously giving access to her spiritual maternity. These two maternities do not exist separately in Mary and it would not be appropriate for it to be otherwise in her heirs.

In any case, the text of December 28, 1936, which I quoted above, clearly indicates that all human generations within the Divine Fiat are called to inherit all the goods of this heavenly mother. This includes both her divine and spiritual motherhood. There is therefore no reason to doubt that an access to the spiritual motherhood of the Virgin Mary does exist within the Divine Fiat.

The spiritual motherhood that little Marys are called to exercise with regard to the faithful implies that they live in an eminent way their common priesthood of the faithful; and thus to be a priestly woman like the Virgin Mary; that by exercising her maternal priesthood.

Indeed, it is one thing to intercede for a group as a member of that group, and it is quite another to do so as the mother of that group. The responsibility of the mother towards her children is greater than that of the children towards each other, and this implies a greater commitment on the part of the Virgin Mary in the exercise of her common priesthood of the faithful.

That being said, it is not part of the duties of the little Mary to administer sacraments or to perform tasks that belong to the ministry of her son-priest. As I mentioned, her ministry consists in exercising the double function of the ministry of the spiritual motherhood of the Virgin Mary : the ministry of maternal intercession within the Divine Fiat and the ministry of spiritual direction within families.

3.4– The evangelical evidence in favor of the reiteration

Now let us look at two very compelling clues within the Gospel that indicate that Christ wants his Church to benefit from the Johannine priestly model.

The first clue is that Christ so closely linked the institution of the Johannine priestly model with our vocation to receive Mary as mother that the one does not go without the other within the scheme of revelation. And this cannot be a coincidence.

Indeed, if Christ had not wanted the Johannine priestly model to be repeated, he could have entrusted his mother to John in private, that is, only in the presence of the other apostles, and this disposition on his part would have been respected by all. He could then have omitted the "Woman, this is your son" at the cross and said only to John: "This is your mother". Thus, each of us would have received the vocation to take Mary as our mother in the order of grace and the particular priestly model of the apostle John could not be repeated.

This choice on his part to link these two elements into a single whole manifests two wishes on his part: the first is that this priestly model be reiterated; the second is that the ministry of the spiritual motherhood of her mother be carried out in tandem with a priest, a tandem that must be lived within a filial type relationship.

Moreover, when we take the trouble to read the words of this vocational pattern with an open mind: "Woman, this is your son» and "This is your mother", we can see that they were pronounced with great authority. In fact, the duality of these words, their brevity and authority evoke the words: "This is my body" "This is my blood". It is possible to say with good reason that they are quasi-sacramental words.

Therefore, is it any wonder that these are the ritual words intended by Christ to reiterate the Johannine priestly model and make possible the exercise of the ministry of the spiritual motherhood of the Virgin Mary within the Church?

The second clue consists in the words he spoke to Peter during his appearance at the shore of Lake Tiberias. Indeed, after his resurrection, after he had told Peter the kind of death by which he was to glorify God, Peter turned around and saw that John was walking behind them. So he said to the Lord, "What about him? implying what will become of him?

This was his answer:

If I want him to stay behind till I come, what does it matter to you? You are to follow me.

(Jn 21, 22)

The next verse adds:

The rumour then went out among the brothers that this disciple would not die. Yet Jesus had not said to Peter, 'He will not die', but, 'If I want him to stay behind till I come'.

(Jn 21, 23)

Tradition indicates that John died in Ephesus at an advanced age. However, this word in verse 22 is, in my opinion, more than a simple expression to signify to Peter that he should mind his own business. It could mean that the apostle John is really called to remain present to his Church until he comes, but not physically, for Christ did not say to Peter, "He shall not die," but "if I want him to stay behind till I come".

However, in order not to prematurely lift the veil on the existence of this priestly model, which he wished to keep in reserve for our time, Christ Jesus kept silent about the mode of presence by which this apostle was called to remain until he came. This silence allowed a rumor to arise in the early Church that the apostle John would not die.

The proof that this rumor was persistent is that John, while writing his gospel some fifty years after this response of Christ to Peter, took the trouble to specify immediately after verse 22 that the Lord had not said that he would not die, but: "If I want him to stay behind till I come." That is how alive this rumor was despite the passage of five decades.

In his omniscience, the risen Christ knew that this enigmatic answer given to Peter would create an unnecessary and persistent rumor within his nascent Church. If he gave it in spite of everything, it was because he really wanted to indicate that John was called to remain present to his Church, but not physically.

Therefore, now that the Johannine priestly model is known to us, it is easy to understand that this presence of John within the Church passes through his very particular priestly model. Therefore, by authorizing the Johannine priestly model two thousand years after its institution by Christ on the cross, the Catholic Church would make John present in the minds of her faithful, through the ordained ministers who would share in his priestly model, until Christ comes.

In my opinion, the recognition of the Johannine priestly model is not an option, but a necessity for two reasons:

- The first is that the traditional priestly model no longer corresponds to the aspirations of the young men of our time. Let us offer them a priestly model filled with reciprocity in Christ; a model where the filial love of Christ Jesus meets the maternal love of Mary making them live the martyrdom of love in the Spirit. If we offer this choice to young Catholic men and women, they will generously respond, "Yes, I am interested in this vocation and its mission!"

- The second is that Mary begat the head of the Church two thousand years ago within the Divine Fiat. She now wants to engender the body of the head (the Church) within this same Fiat. How can this be done? Through the pastoral ministry that the Johannine priestly model will carry out within families, making them domestic Churches within the Divine Fiat.

3.5– In order to avoid the risk of scandal

If, in accordance with the spirituality I propose for this priestly model [1], the truth is done and the spirituality of the Divine Will is integrated with the paternal or maternal pole that the Johannine priestly model implies, then, the reign of God being firmly established in these souls, there should be no risk of scandal.

However, in order to avoid the insidious gossip that could engender the fact that a nun lives under the same roof as a priest, nothing prevents little Marie from having separate accommodation from her son-priest.

Indeed, the fact that this nun is under the protection of her son-priest does not imply, strictly speaking, that she must live under the same roof as him. The important thing is that she joins him at the beginning of the day, so that they can live with one heart in the Divine Fiat, starting with the morning liturgy of the hours, the various tasks and activities of their daily life. And this is without mentioning their pastoral ministry within families that they will have to carry out together.

---

1 See the bibliography at the end of this document

In any case, it is up to the Church to discern and issue the norms regarding the morals and customs to be adopted with regard to this priestly model, if it decides to repeat it.

3.6– The two pillars

At the end of this analysis, it is possible to affirm that the Johannine priestly model rests on two pillars. If one of these is missing, then it cannot be repeated. These two pillars are:

The first pillar consists in determining whether a bishop can, by the power of binding and loosing that he received at his episcopal ordination, entrust a nun to a priest so that she can exercise a pastoral ministry in connection with him.

As for the second pillar, it consists in confirming the access to the divine and spiritual motherhood of the Virgin Mary in the spirituality of the Divine Will.

4

Various

In this last section, I bring together various points that deserve our attention. Namely, the spirituality that I suggest for this priestly model and my recommendations for the spiritual direction of his seminarians.

But before look at them without delay, I would like to add that the little Marys, although they are religious, should not have a distinctive habit. They will only wear a chain or a ring with an M surmounted by a cross as a sign of their religious consecration. This must be so, because it is necessary that married women and young girls can identify with them. May their dress be at the same time chaste, dignified and simple. They must be a model for all women in this respect. And let it be the ardent maternal love that they will have towards all that distinguishes them from other women.

4.1– Spiritual formation and its importance

The formation of those who could be called to take part in this priestly model implies the integration of a strong spirituality. Otherwise, it should not be repeated.

Only a proper integration of the spirituality of the Divine Will can adequately preserve the Johannine priestly model from any risk of scandal or corruption. Once integrated, this spirituality would make this priestly model less at risk than the traditional priestly model without this spirituality.

As we have seen, in order to be faithful to their vocation, little Johns and little Marys will have to exercise the spiritual fatherhood of Christ and the spiritual motherhood of Mary, respectively, within the Divine Fiat. The integration of this spirituality is necessary because of these two poles which are indispensable for the Johannine priestly model.

Indeed, even if Saint John could not live within the Divine Fiat, the gift of the Divine Fiat not being available at the time, the fact remains that he lived his apostolic ministry under the pole of fatherhood. We need only read his first letter in the Catholic epistles to discover this. In this letter, which contains only five short chapters, he addresses the recipients of his letter seven times using the terms "children" or "little children".

Through the book entitled: *Celui qui fait la vérité vient à la lumière*, I indicate the spirituality that the Spirit of the Lord has taught me so that those who are destined for this priestly model may do the truth, that is, reach adoration in the spirit, which I compare to the stage of spiritual betrothal with Christ Jesus.

In my opinion, the acquisition of worship in spirit is the best preparation for entering the spirituality of the Divine Will. It is possible to teach the Divine Will to the laity without them having previously done the truth, but I can only recommend very strongly that the acquisition of adoration in spirit be achieved before beginning the integration of the Divine Will in the seminarians (men and women) who would be destined to this priestly model.

Of course, I leave it to Mother Church to discern the appropriateness of the spirituality I propose for this priestly model. However, I tenderly implore that no one be admitted to this priestly model, on the one hand, until that soul has does the truth about itself and, on the other, until it has adequately integrated the spirituality of the Divine Will.

4.2– Spiritual direction and vocational discernment

Since this priestly model requires a spiritual formation that may take longer than the traditional priestly model, I strongly suggest that it be carried out within a religious congregation; a congregation whose function would be to prepare seminarians, both men and women, to integrate this priestly model and its spirituality.

Here are my suggestions for the spiritual direction and vocational discernment of seminarians in this congregation:

- The Church of the place where this seminary will be established and, eventually, this congregation will put their best elements of life in spirit (contemplation and prayer), wisdom, intelligence, discernment, knowledge of human nature in charge of the spiritual direction of the seminarians. They will form the very select committee for spiritual direction and vocational discernment. This committee will be composed of men and women: men for the spiritual direction of young men and women for the spiritual direction of young women.

- This committee will begin by developing a plan for spiritual direction and vocational discernment, ensuring that it is as complete and adapted as possible to the spirituality of this priestly model and to what it requires. In developing this plan, they will be inspired by the best practices in this area within the Church and will adapt it to the requirements of the Johannine priestly model.

The purpose of this plan will be to provide a framework for spiritual direction to foster worship in spirit and truth and after the integration of the

Divine Will, to homogenize the teachings that enable this journey from one spiritual director to the next, and to assist in the discernment of the vocation of seminarians.

- Once this plan is established, they will follow it faithfully and improve it over time.

Because of their extensive knowledge of the seminarians for whom they provide spiritual direction, it is appropriate that they be involved in decisions regarding the pairing men and women seminarians. Such pairings should not take place until the stage of worship in spirit and in truth is reached.

Of course, in addition to a strong catechesis, the intellectual formation of the seminarian who is destined to be a little John must correspond to that of the traditional priestly model. As for those who are destined to be little Marys, they should receive a solid formation in catechesis, "oratio", spirituality of the Divine Will, spiritual direction and family dynamics. In short, everything that is essential to know in order to make Christian families domestic churches.

May I ask that emphasis be placed on reading and on the production of essays or reading summaries within the intellectual formation of those who are destined to do so? There is nothing better than reading and the spiritual exercise called "oratio" for the acquisition and integration of theological knowledge and writing for the development of reflective skills.

After their intellectual formation, I strongly recommend that they be given a certain amount of time (two to three years) so that they can receive themselves in the intuitions of their soul; this is essential in order to become an authentic Master of the Word. This applies equally to seminarians - men or women. However, if concessions are to be made, this recommendation will apply only to the future priest. They will thus be able to appropriate divine revelation in a way that is both personal and in keeping with Tradition.

Those who are destined to take part in the priestly model of the Apostle John must have a good interiority, which includes a good capacity for concentration. If they are not capable of this type of formation, they should not be admitted to the Johannine priestly model.

If they are not humanly and spiritually ready after the time of their formation, they will live the religious life that corresponds to the needs of this congregation. And, if one day they prove to be ready, then they will be integrated.

Because of the countless scandals involving homosexuality among the clergy in the not too distant past, I feel compelled to state that a person with homosexual tendencies, man or woman, cannot be integrated into the Johannine priestly model. The same is true for a person who, like me, carries a deep emotional wound.

Indeed, a man with homosexual tendencies does not have what it takes to exercise the fatherhood and authority that the ministry of the priesthood requires. The same goes for a woman with these tendencies, she cannot have the necessary interior dispositions to exercise the ministry of the spiritual motherhood of the Virgin Mary.

In saying this, I am not in any way denigrating those people for whom the discovery of this state of affairs is usually a profound tragedy, but things must be said.

So, let no one be unduly hurt by not having what it takes to take part in the Johannine priestly model, because the Lord loves each of his children and has a vocation tailored to each of them. Let them know that their happiness will blossom when the Lord makes known to them the magnificent vocation that is theirs.

4.3– An ombudsman for the protection of seminarians

It is essential that seminarians have access to an ombudsman to prevent sexual misconduct or abuse of authority within the seminary. This ombudsman must be of exemplary integrity and have the skills necessary to investigate complaints.

It is equally essential that he or she have the power to demand the replacement of a person in authority within the seminary, if he or she deems it appropriate: it does not matter if it is a superior or a member of the committee on spiritual direction and vocational discernment. If, after investigation, the respondent cannot be entirely exonerated of the alleged facts, especially if they involve a sexual proposition or gesture, he or she should be removed from the seminary and replaced by another on whom there is no suspicion.

Therefore, the ombudsman must be independent of the seminary and of the religious community of the Johannine priestly model. He should therefore be answerable only to the local bishop or to the papal authority from whom he would receive his remuneration.

Conclusion

At the end of this reflection, I believe that I have demonstrated that what I am announcing concerning the Johannine priestly model is plausible and that it deserves to be examined in theological and ecclesial circles.

This plausibility derives from the particular vocation addressed to John and Mary within the schema in Jn 19, 26-27 and thanks to the access to the spiritual motherhood of the Virgin Mary within the Divine Will.

These two vocations come from the word: "Woman, this is your son," in which Mary is entrusted to John and John is called to receive her filially, as a son takes his mother into his home. As a result, they exercised together their pastoral ministries in the early Church.

The evangelical episode of the wedding at Cana and that of Golgotha have allowed us to see that the Johannine priestly model must be lived within the Divine Fiat and more specifically by assuming the spiritual fatherhood of Christ (for the priest) and the divine and spiritual motherhood of the Virgin Mary (for the religious woman). As for the pastoral ministry of this priestly model, it would have as its goal to make of these families domestic churches, that is to say, places where Christ Jesus would be adored and his word welcomed and lived out daily. All this within the Divine Fiat.

Thus, thanks to the teachings of their little Mary, married women will learn to exercise within the Divine Fiat the double function of Mary's maternal priesthood within their family. As for married men, thanks to the teaching of their little John, they will learn to exercise the spiritual fatherhood of Christ within this same Fiat.

Indeed, without in any way denigrating the traditional priestly model, I believe that the Johannine priestly model would be much more adapted to family ministry, because couples could identify with their little John and their little Mary and take them as models.

I conclude by mentioning that I am deeply convinced that the Johannine priestly model and its mission within families will not be foreign to the triumph of the Immaculate Heart of Mary. How could this priestly model contribute to the triumph of her Heart? Through the ministry of little Marys who would reveal in a sensitive way the maternal love of her Heart to the Church and to the world.

Yes, we know that the predominant virtue within the Immaculate Heart of Mary is love, but more precisely maternal love. That is why the revelation of her maternal love, through the ministry of the little Marys, could contribute greatly to the triumph of her Immaculate Heart.

Biographie de l'auteur

Femme, voici ton fils. Voici ta mère.

(Roman catholique proposant un modèle sacerdotal inédit)

Celui qui fait la vérité vient à la lumière

(Spiritualité à l'intention du modèle sacerdotal johannique)

Paper version:

Pending publication by a Catholic publisher, this book is available on your local amazon site.

Digital version:

This book is sold for a small fee in EPUB format at the following site: https ://www.kobo.com

www.ingramcontent.com/pod-product-compliance
Lightning Source LLC
La Vergne TN
LVHW050620200726
843508LV00010B/1939